1994 Edition
Published by Wishing Well Books,
an imprint of Joshua Morris Publishing, Inc.,
221 Danbury Road, Wilton, CT 06897.
Copyright © 1986 The Five Mile Press Pty. Ltd.
All rights reserved. Printed in Singapore.
ISBN: 0-88705-749-7
10 9 8 7 6 5 4 3 2 1

Rupert Takes a Bath

BOB GRAHAM

WISHING WELL BOOKS

Here is a blue bathtub.

Here is James in the bathtub.

He can poke up his knees
like two pink islands . . .

and the water comes up
to his middle.

Here is his dog, Rupert.

Rupert wants the duck.

Look out, James!

In goes Rupert.

Look! Now the water is up
to James's neck.

When Rupert gets out, the
water will go down again.

Here is the water with
Rupert and James.

Here is the water with just James.

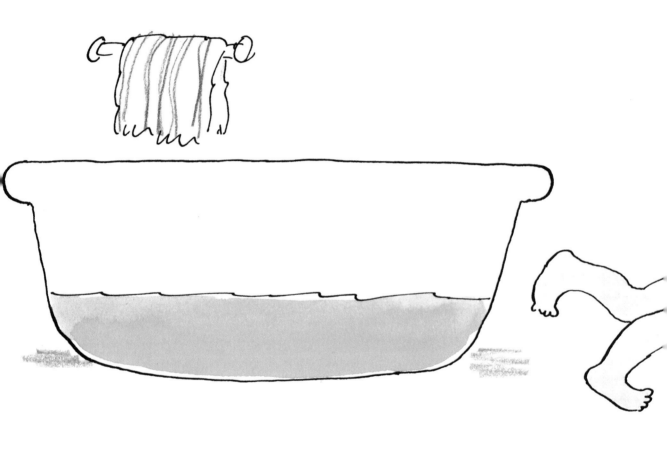

Look where the water is now . . .
without James.

water

Water will take the shape of its container. The amount of space an object (in this case, James) occupies is known as the volume of the object. The volume of an object will cause a displacement of water. If the object floats, the displacement of water will be equal in weight to that of the object. This is known as Archimedes' Principle.

Experiments to try

1. Fill two identical glasses halfway with water, so that each glass contains the same amount of water. Have your child mark the water level on the outside of each glass. Place a small potato in the first glass and place a larger potato in the second glass. Have your child note the difference in the water levels.

2. Fill a container right to the brim. Ask your child to place a large object—one that will sink—into the container. What happens? Try it again with an object that will float. Does the same thing happen?